COOL SCIENCE

SPARE PARTS
for People

Michael C. Harris

mc Marshall Cavendish
Benchmark
New York

This edition first published in 2011 in the United States
by Marshall Cavendish Benchmark.

Marshall Cavendish Benchmark
99 White Plains Road
Tarrytown, NY 10591
www.marshallcavendish.us

Copyright © 2011 Q2AMedia

Published by Marshall Cavendish Benchmark
An imprint of Marshall Cavendish Corporation

Other Marshall Cavendish Offices:
Marshall Cavendish International (Asia) Private Limited, 1 New Industrial Road, Singapore 536196
• Marshall Cavendish International (Thailand) Co Ltd. 253 Asoke, 12th Flr, Sukhumvit 21 Road, Klongtoey Nua,
Wattana, Bangkok 10110, Thailand • Marshall Cavendish (Malaysia) Sdn Bhd, Times Subang,
Lot 46, Subang Hi-Tech Industrial Park, Batu Tiga, 40000 Shah Alam,
Selangor Darul Ehsan, Malaysia

Marshall Cavendish is a trademark of Times Publishing Limited

Library of Congress Cataloging-in-Publication Data
Harris, Michael C. (Michael Christopher), 1963-
Spare parts for people / Michael C. Harris.
p. cm. – (Cool science)
Includes index.
ISBN 978-1-60870-080-6
1. Artificial organs–Juvenile literature. 2. Artificial limbs–Juvenile
literature. 3. Implants, Artificial–Juvenile literature. I. Title.
RD130.H37 2011
617.9'5–dc22
2009053776

Created by Q2AMedia
Series Editor: Bonnie Dobkin
Art Director: Harleen Mehta
Client Service Manager: Santosh Vasudevan
Project Manager: Kumar Kunal
Line Artist: Manoj Sharma, Martin James
Coloring Artists: Manoj Sharma, Shubhendu Karmaker
Photo research: Sujatha Menon
Designers: Neha Kaul, Parul Gambhir

The photographs in this book are used by permission and through the courtesy of:

Cover: Michael Svoboda/Shutterstock, Shutterstock, Natalia Siverina/Shutterstock
Half title: Shutterstock

4: Sophia Winters/Fotolia; 6: Science Museum/Science & Society Picture Library; 7: Library of Congress Prints and Photographs Division
Washington, D.C.; 8: Roger Dale Pleis/Shutterstock; 9: Kevin A Somerville/Photolibrary; 10l: Urs Flueeler/Keystone/AP Photo;
10r: Michael Svoboda/123RF; 11: Andy Fossum/Rex Features; 12: Michael Courtney/Istockphoto; 13: Win McNamee & Staff/Getty Images;
14: South West News Service; 15: Gene J. Puskar/AP Photo; 16: The Circle of Ancient Iranian Studies (CAIS); 17: Dr. Isaac Lipshitz/
VisionCare Opthalmic Technologies, Inc.; 19: Bandika/Fotolia; 20: Claudia Daut/Reuters; 21: Cochlear Ltd; 22: Mike Devlin/Science
Photolibrary; 23: Science Limited/Photolibrary; 25: Denis Charlet/AFP; 27: Don Farrall/Photolibrary; 28: ©Texas Heart Institute
www.texasheart.org; 29t: Abiomed, Inc.; 29b: Forrest Anderson/AP Photo; 30: David Parker/Science Photo Library; 31t: Duane R.Miller/
AP Photo; 31c: Eric Isselée/Istockphoto; 32: Beerkoff/Fotolia; 33: Eliandric/Istockphoto; 34: Krishna Kumar/Big Stock Photo;
35: Shutterstock; 36: Photolibrary; 37: Chris Klug; 38: Regentec Limited; 39: Ruslan Dashinsky/Istockphoto; 40: Frederick M. Brown/
Getty Images; 41: Integrated Defense Systems Raytheon Company; 43: Sebastian Kaulitzki/Shutterstock;
44: Wake Forest Institute for Regenerative Medicine; 45: Istockphoto

Q2AMedia Art Bank: 5, 17, 18, 19, 24, 26, 42

Printed in Malaysia (T)

135642

4831

CONTENTS

BODY PARTS

Bionic hearts. Eye telescopes. Brain implants. Do these words make you think of some strange human-machine hybrid from the future? Well, that future is now.

We humans are benefiting from hundreds of inventions that have given us our very own replacement parts. Arms, knees, kidneys, heart valves, and blood vessels can all be replaced. Even the brain can be repaired!

Human or Machine?

A body part can be replaced either organically or artificially. An **organic** replacement means that a healthy body part or organ is used to replace an unhealthy one. For example, if a person's kidneys are failing, doctors will remove the healthy kidney from a donor and transplant it into the person whose kidneys have failed. There have even been cases where animal organs taken from baboons and pigs—have been transplanted into human bodies.

Artificial replacement parts don't come from another person or an animal. They usually come from research laboratories or medical supply companies. In recent decades, there have been great advances in artificial body part equipment. Much of that is due to computers and electronic technology. As both have become more powerful, inventors have been able to use that science to create electronic-based replacement parts, usually called **bionic** parts. These can range from hands that respond to electronic **impulses** from the user's nerve endings to exciting new ways to help restore people's eyesight.

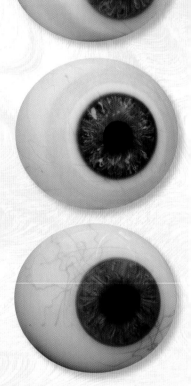

Artificial eyes can look identical to real ones.

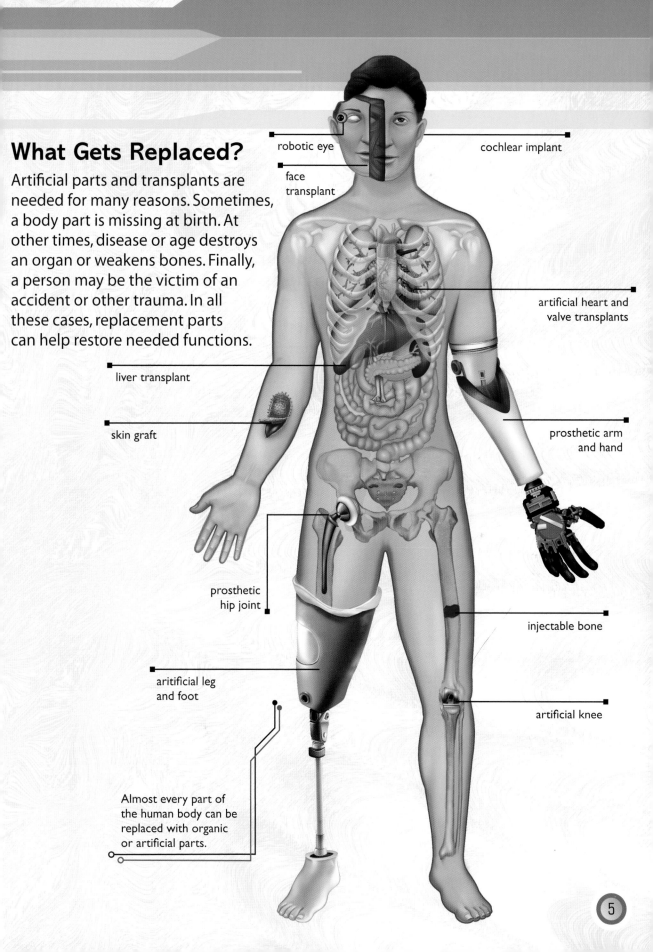

What Gets Replaced?

Artificial parts and transplants are needed for many reasons. Sometimes, a body part is missing at birth. At other times, disease or age destroys an organ or weakens bones. Finally, a person may be the victim of an accident or other trauma. In all these cases, replacement parts can help restore needed functions.

robotic eye

face transplant

cochlear implant

artificial heart and valve transplants

liver transplant

skin graft

prosthetic arm and hand

prosthetic hip joint

injectable bone

aritificial leg and foot

artificial knee

Almost every part of the human body can be replaced with organic or artificial parts.

WOODEN TOES, LEAD TEETH

Humans have been experimenting with artificial body parts for thousands of years. In fact, the oldest known artificial leg was discovered in Capua, Italy. It was used in Roman times around the year 300 BCE!

People continued to experiment with artificial parts—limbs, eyes, noses, and teeth—throughout history. The same craftsmen who hammered out suits of armor for knights also made **prostheses**. They often used iron to create fake arms and legs. The replacement parts were heavy, but they worked.

This is a copy of the "Capua leg," which was made of copper and wood. It was discovered in a Roman grave.

THEN AND NOW

In 2007, scientists revealed what may be the oldest working artificial body part ever found: a wooden false toe from a mummy currently on display in Cairo, Egypt. Believed to be three thousand years old, the sections of the wooden toe are held together by strips of leather that served as joints. The bottom and sides of the toe show wear and tear, which means this Cairo resident really did use it to walk around town!

But some of the biggest advances in artificial body parts came during and after the Civil War (1861–1865), when tens of thousands of soldiers had arms or legs amputated. The terrible number of wounded soldiers spurred great innovation in the design of prostheses. Instead of iron, replacement limbs were now made of lightweight wood and sometimes had bendable knees and elbows. The science of artificial body parts would soar to amazing heights over the next one hundred years. Even more dramatic changes would follow once computer technology became part of the scientific mix.

INSIDE KNOWLEDGE

America's first president, George Washington, was plagued with bad teeth. (In fact, for much of his adult life he only had one tooth.) Washington's lack of teeth caused him great pain, and he was very self-conscious. So he wore different sets of fake teeth, or dentures, made from human, horse, and donkey teeth. He also had teeth made of ivory and lead. Despite a famous myth, however, he never had wooden teeth!

This set of false teeth was worn by President George Washington. They must have been very uncomfortable!

Legs, Hips, and Joints

Artificial legs have been around since before pirates used peg legs. Today's versions, though, are like nothing those pirates could ever have imagined!

Over the past century, the materials used for prosthetic legs have become lighter, more flexible, and more like real limbs. Plastic is the most widely used material, along with titanium, aluminum, and carbon fiber. These materials are durable, can hold a lot of weight, and can easily be customized to fit the amputee's body.

Materials like carbon fiber have made artificial limbs lighter than ever before.

The Right Fit

The most challenging aspect of fitting someone for an artificial leg is the socket—where the artificial leg meets the remaining real leg. Legs can be attached with suction socks, straps, or long bolts or screws that are implanted directly into the end of the person's leg stump. Scientists are also making some amazing advances in **myoelectricity**. This method uses electrical impulses from the muscle to move the artificial limb.

Hips and Joints

Roughly one million people a year have hip or knee replacement surgery. Athletes are frequently candidates for such surgeries, but so are elderly people with arthritis and brittle bones. The procedure involves attaching the replacement part directly to the patient's bone. Materials such as titanium, cobalt-chrome, and polyethylene are used to attach the limb because they are strong and biocompatible.

INSIDE KNOWLEDGE

Did you know that an artificial knee is made up of the same material found on the space shuttle and in plastic grocery bags? Cobalt-chrome, used on the shuttle, is a strong metal that is highly heat-resistant. Polyethylene, the plastic bag material, is strong and very flexible—just what a knee should be!

This prosthetic hip joint mimics the shape and function of the actual joint as much as possible.

JUST AMAZING!

Prosthetic technology is becoming more and more advanced. The Power Knee, for example, uses electronic sensors to gauge the person's weight, balance, and stride. This helps prevent users from falling or losing balance and greatly increases their walking speed.

Oscar Pistorius: Fastest Man on No Legs

South Africa native Oscar Pistorius was born with bones missing from his lower legs. The legs were amputated when Pistorius was barely a year old. Despite this, Pistorius became an Olympic-class runner.

Pistorius has mastered running on Cheetah Blades, J-shaped carbon fiber prostheses designed by an Icelandic company. The blades are flexible enough to withstand the weight and movement of a runner who is pushing forward.

Pistorius originally set his sights on the 2008 Summer Olympics in Beijing but failed to make the team. Undaunted, the "Blade Runner" is now in training for the 2012 Summer Olympics in London.

Cheetah Blades are custom-built to meet each runner's specific needs.

Some able-bodied runners complained that Pistorius's blades gave him an unfair advantage in races.

Aimee Mullins: Brains, Beauty, and Prostheses

"What does a beautiful woman have to look like?" asks Aimee Mullins. She believes women can be beautiful, even if they have prostheses. A double-amputee since childhood, Mullins has spent most of her adult life changing the way people think about artificial body parts and beauty.

Aimee Mullins is an accomplished athlete. In college, using Cheetah Blades, she set Paralympics records in both the 100-meter dash and the long jump.

Mullins has modeled clothes at fashion shows in London, and has been featured in high fashion print ads. She is an actor as well, and frequently travels the world as a motivational speaker. She brings a dozen of her artificial limbs onstage so audiences can see her change into different sets of legs.

11

Arms and Hands

In *Peter Pan*, Captain Hook's artificial hand was used mainly to threaten other pirates and scare small children. But the hook concept started what would become an amazing revolution in artificial limbs.

The split-hook hand, first designed in 1912, has been used by amputees ever since. It's lightweight, it makes gripping items easy, and it doesn't cost a lot to repair. Special gloves cover the hooks to make them look more like hands. Other types of hands and arms have been made of wood, plastic, metal, and carbon fiber. Until recently, the fake limbs only moved at the elbows or wrists. But with advances in computers and **nanotechnology**, today's bionic arms move in surprisingly lifelike ways.

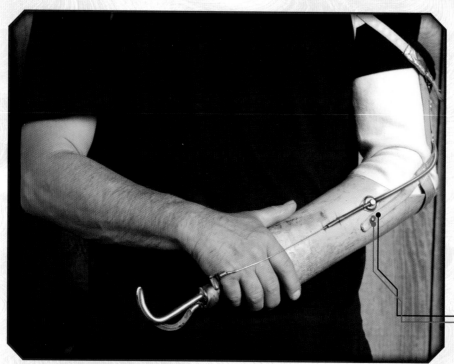

Split-hook hands are light, inexpensive, and durable.

The Utah Revolution

In the 1970s, scientists at the University of Utah developed the first myoelectric arm. It has a special interface on the end that picks up the electronic impulses from the remaining muscles of the patient's arm.

Computer programs then translate these impulses into commands to make the motorized fingers and thumb move. Now all someone with an artificial arm or hand needs to do is think about moving and the limb goes into action!

Getting Real

Researchers aren't willing to stop with the success of artificial limbs, no matter how well they work. Now they are experimenting with transplanting actual body parts. Hands and forearms have been successfully transplanted, and other body parts won't be far behind.

INSIDE KNOWLEDGE

Scientists are now learning how to give artificial hands a sense of touch. Doctors attach the nerve endings that used to extend into the patient's real arm or hand to an electronic device attached to the chest. The device is then connected to the tips of the artificial fingers. People who have had this experimental operation have found that they can feel temperature and pain in their bionic fingers.

Claudia Mitchell demonstrates the use of her thought-controlled bionic arm.

Evan Reynolds: Getting A Grip

Evan Reynolds's left arm was dangling outside of a car window when he drove too close to a fence post. His hand was cut off and his life changed in an instant. Thanks to a Scottish company's revolutionary i-LIMB bionic hand, nineteen-year-old Reynolds soon had a replacement hand—the closest thing to a real hand that science could imagine. Each finger of the i-LIMB has its own motor. The whole hand is powered by a rechargeable battery that sits in the socket where the hand meets Reynolds's arm stump. The hand uses the electric pulses from Reynolds's arm muscles to make the fingers and thumb move. What's most remarkable about the i-LIMB is its gripping ability. It can easily hold everything from a heavy cup to a thin piece of paper. Reynolds can even peel an apple!

Reynolds says that within minutes, he was able to use his prosthetic hand as well as he does now.

Jeff Kepner: Give Him A Hand Or Two!

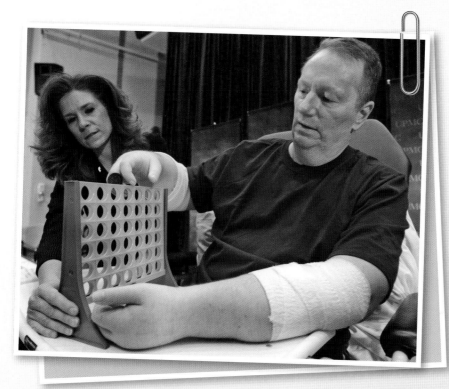

If all goes well, Jeff Kepner will be clapping for his daughter when she graduates from high school. He just won't be clapping with his own hands. In May of 2009, Kepner became the first person in the United States to receive a double hand transplant.

Years ago, Kepner lost both legs and hands to a bacterial infection. He learned to use his split-hook hands expertly, but then donor hands

Kepner is already able to use his hands to pick up small objects like game pieces.

became available. The nine-hour double hand-transplant surgery was risky, but successful. After just a few months of physical therapy, Kepner was already able to move his new fingers. Additional therapy will help strengthen the muscles in his transplanted hands, letting the nerves grow slowly but surely.

EYE TO EYE

Sight is the sense most people depend on most. Any loss of vision can change a person's life dramatically. Thanks to science, though, the loss often doesn't have to be permanent.

The eye is one of the most complicated organs in the human body. For centuries, scientists have struggled to come up with solutions for loss of sight.

Better than a Patch

When someone loses an eye—to cancer, in battle, or because of an accident—the eye is usually replaced with an artificial one. In the past, these eyes were made of wood or glass. Today, plastic is the most commonly used material. In most cases, the entire eye isn't replaced. The prosthetic eye is a thin, hard plastic shell that is fitted to the person's eye socket. These shells don't help the user see, but they do help people feel more confident about how they look.

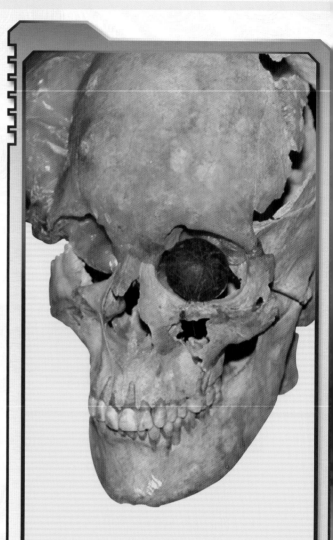

JUST AMAZING!

In 2006, archaeologists in Iran discovered the oldest known artificial eyeball. The 4,800-year-old eye belonged to a young woman and was made of tar and animal fat. It was painted white, and there was a clear pupil marked in the center. The eye was attached to the socket with gold wires.

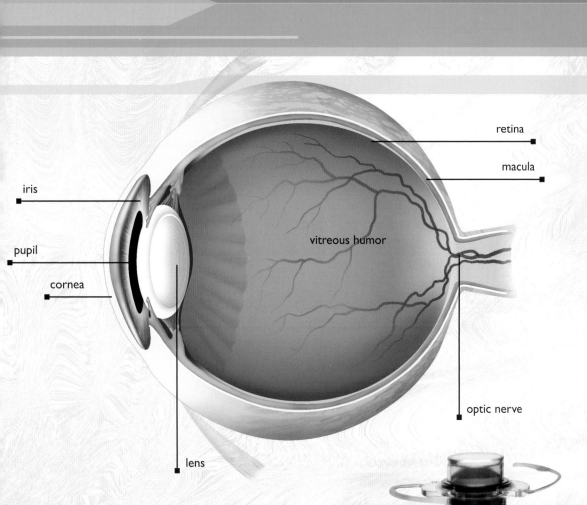

retina

macula

iris

pupil

cornea

vitreous humor

optic nerve

lens

Transplants and Telescopes

Older people often have trouble with their sight. Sometimes, the cornea of the eye—the clear part of the eye in front of the iris and pupil—becomes damaged or diseased. When that happens, doctors can actually transplant corneal tissue from someone who has recently died.

People may also suffer from macular degeneration. This disease causes blurred vision, blind spots, and general dimming of the light one sees. Strange as it sounds, a person with macular degeneration can be helped by a tiny telescope that is inserted behind the iris. The telescope magnifies what the person is looking at, improving his or her ability to see.

This implantable miniature telescope (IMT), is placed behind the pupil and sends images to the retina.

INSIDE KNOWLEDGE

Chinese scientists have developed a robotic eye that moves in unison with the remaining real eye. Tiny electrodes are placed in each eye socket. As the real eye moves, the electrodes send those movements to the robotic eye so it can move in the same way.

Ron's Bionic Eye

After thirty years of seeing nothing but black, seventy-three-year-old Ron is able to see light and objects around him. His bionic eye, which he received in 2008, works this way: a tiny video camera and microprocessor on a specially designed pair of glasses wirelessly send the images to a receiver on the outside of the eye. The receiver then sends the information to electrodes implanted at the back of the eye. These electrodes send the images directly to the brain. All this happens in less than a second. Ron and the other eighteen patients who received these bionic eyes can only see from one eye, and everything is in black and white. But after years of darkness, color can wait.

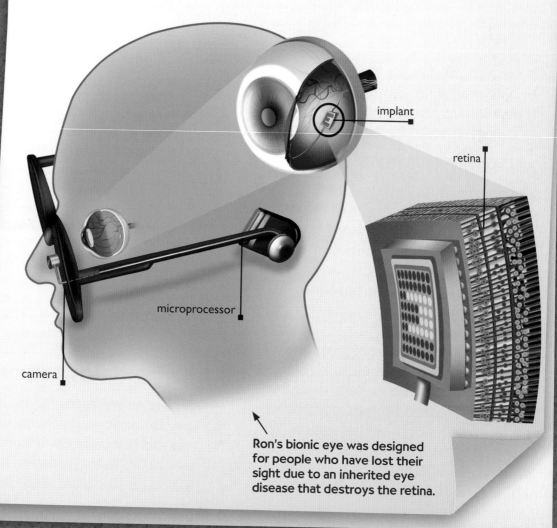

implant

retina

microprocessor

camera

Ron's bionic eye was designed for people who have lost their sight due to an inherited eye disease that destroys the retina.

HEAR, HEAR!

What's the most common way people deal with hearing loss? That's right—by telling others to SPEAK UP! Luckily, science and technology have come up with much better (and quieter) solutions.

The first solution to hearing loss was the hearing aid. The idea behind a hearing aid is that the sound is amplified, or increased, by a receiver that picks up sound and directs it right into the ear canal.

Hearing aids used to be big and awkward, with cords running from a microphone box to the person's ears. Today, they are much smaller and less noticeable. Some aids have a hard plastic case that sits behind the ear, and a tube that runs into the ear canal. Other hearing aids sit in the opening of the ear canal. There's even a hearing aid that sits inside the ear canal, where nobody can see it.

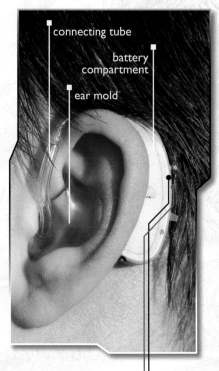

connecting tube

battery compartment

ear mold

In addition to the parts you can see, all hearing aids contain a microphone that turns sounds into electrical impulses, and a speaker that sends those impulses to the brain.

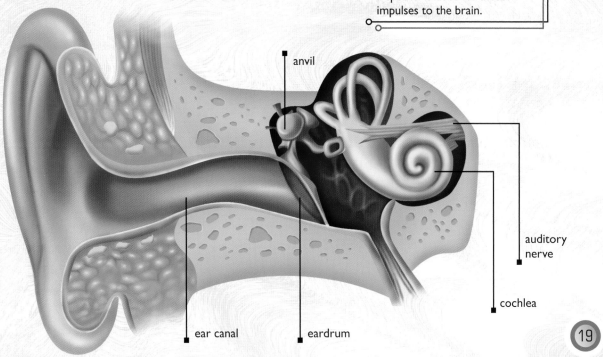

anvil

auditory nerve

cochlea

ear canal

eardrum

Your Skull Can Hear, Too

The Bone Anchored Hearing Aid (BAHA) is used by people whose outer and middle ears don't work properly. The idea behind the BAHA system is to bypass those parts of the ear.

A titanium screw is surgically implanted into the bone near the ear. After a few months, when the skull bone has healed, a battery-operated receiver is attached to the screw. The receiver picks up sounds and sends them through the screw into the bone. The vibrations in the bone go directly to the nerves in the inner ear to reproduce sound.

Breaking the Silence

Like the BAHA, a cochlear implant uses a receiver and transmitter to capture sound and send it to the inner ear. These implants are used by people who have very severe hearing problems or who can't hear at all.

The implants are attached to the inside and outside of the skull behind the ear. An electric wire is installed directly into the cochlea, which is the part of the inner ear that turns sound vibrations into electric signals that the brain can understand. It takes a while for people with cochlear implants to learn how to hear with them. That's because the sound is not as sharp or clear as it is for those with normal hearing. But for many users, cochlear implants shatter the wall of silence they have been living with.

The disc on this boy's head is actually a cochlear implant. No part of the actual ear is involved.

THEN AND NOW

Until the early twentieth century, the ear trumpet was the best solution for people with hearing loss. It was shaped like a tube or horn, and it amplified sound. The small end went in the person's ear canal and the speaker spoke loudly at the wide end. Simple, yes, but effective!

Sarah Novick: Learning to Hear

When Sarah was seven months old, her parents noticed she wasn't babbling or gurgling like other children her age. At eleven months, her hearing was tested. The little girl was almost completely deaf.

Hearing aids didn't help much. Sarah was slow to develop speech or language skills because she couldn't hear. When she was eighteen months old, Sarah received her first cochlear implant. As soon as it was activated, she started reacting to sounds. Within six months, she was responding to words, phrases, and songs.

When she was five and a half, Sarah received a second implant. Today, she can talk on the phone for hours or listen to her favorite music—just like any other kid!

The rounded part of a device like this one is attached to Sarah's skull. The other section fits over her ear.

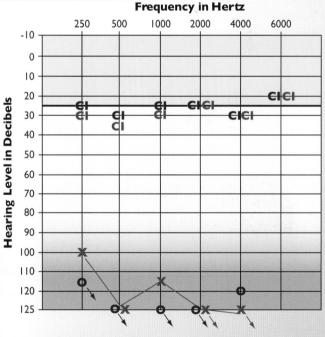

This chart shows the improvement in Sarah's hearing after the implants.

O-Pre-implant, right ear, **X**-Pre-implant, left ear
CI-After cochlear implant, right ear
CI-After cochlear implant, left ear

Skin and Tissue

Skin is the largest organ of the human body, and it's a tough substance! Finding a material strong enough to replace human skin has been a challenge for researchers. Recently, artificial skin and tissue have been getting stronger and more lifelike.

When skin is scraped or slightly torn, the body does a great job of growing more skin to heal the wound. Still, big scrapes or larger **abrasions** sometimes require a skin graft to repair the area.

To do a skin graft, skin is peeled off one section of the body (usually the hips or legs or buttocks) and sewn over the damaged area. Usually the skin comes from the person needing the transplant. Sometimes, though, doctors use skin from someone else, usually a relative, whose skin is less likely to be rejected by the patient's immune system than that of a stranger. The grafted skin easily fuses with the skin surrounding the injury.

This skin graft is almost completely healed. Full recovery can take several months or more.

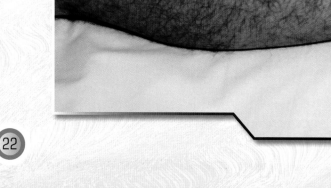

Artificial Skin

Skin grafts work well for small areas. However, when people suffer severe burns all over their body or survive certain devastating forms of cancer, the body simply can't make skin fast enough to heal itself.

In the 1970s, two chemistry professors created the first usable artificial skin, called Silastic®. It looked more like mesh than skin, and it was made from shark cartilage and cow **collagen**. With large sheets of Silastic, doctors were able to help patients with severely burned skin heal faster. As the patient's own skin grew back, the shark and cow elements were absorbed by the body.

Scientists are working on other ideas as well. One research group is developing a self-repairing plastic skin that bleeds and heals itself. Australian and Korean researchers have created a spongy artificial tissue made from human DNA that may one day be used to replace skin, muscle, tendons, and possibly even arteries.

Surviving skin from a burn victim can be removed and grown in a culture. It is then placed over the burn area.

INSIDE KNOWLEDGE

German scientists have created a complex artificial skin with working blood vessels. This could be a major improvement in treating burn victims, who often need a large amount of new skin. Starting with actual skin cells, the process uses computer automation to reduce human contact keep everything sterile, and create the skin more efficiently.

Isabelle Dinoire's New Face

In 2005, a dog attacked Isabelle Dinoire and tore off part of her nose, lips, cheeks, and mouth. She was left unable to speak, and had to be fed through a tube.

Six months later, after an innovative new transplant surgery, Dinoire became the world's first successful recipient of a partial-face transplant.

The team of surgeons who performed the operation used tissue from a brain-dead donor to replace the bottom half of Dinoire's face. Skin, lips, muscles, and nerves were all part of the triangle-shaped patch that was used. In addition, bone marrow cells were injected to keep Dinoire's body from rejecting the new skin. Never before had so much facial skin and tissue been transplanted from one person to another.

The transplant replaced a section of Dinoire's face that began halfway up the bridge of her nose and continued through the cheek area and below her chin.

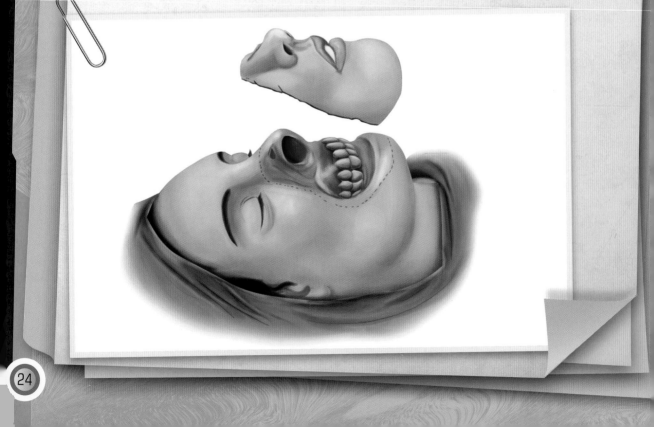

Slow Road to Smiles

The mouth and lips were the most difficult parts of the transplant process. They not only had to look good, but they had to work properly. It took nearly a year of nerve and tissue growth, as well as physical therapy, for Dinoire to be able to control the muscles around her lips and mouth soshe could speak clearly and eat without problems.

Despite the overall success, the transplant did create some serious side effects. At one point, Isabelle experienced kidney failure due to infection. There were also two episodes of skin rejection, which doctors were able to control with drugs. Isabelle will have to take those drugs for the rest of her life.

There was also a change in her appearance. Dinoire's original face had a wide, tilted nose, thin lips, and a strong jaw. The new face has a thinner nose, fuller lips, and a more rounded jaw. Dinoire commented that it was sometimes strange to see someone else's face when she looked in the mirror.

Nearly two years after the surgery, once the healing process was complete, Dinoire met with the media and the world saw the results of her surgery. She has been an inspiration to transplant patients ever since.

Over time, Dinoire's scars began to fade. She also is able to control the muscles of her face.

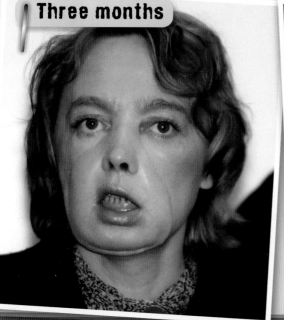

Three months

One year

Hearts, Blood, and Vessels

It's hard to imagine replacements for parts as important as the heart, blood, and blood vessels. Yet doctors and researchers have been working on them for decades.

The first human heart transplant took place in 1967 in South Africa. The patient only lived for eighteen days, but today, patients can live for decades after the transplant.

A heart transplant is performed when someone's heart can no longer do its job. A donor heart is located and brought to the hospital. The patient is hooked up to a cardiopulmonary bypass machine—a heart and lung machine that keeps the patient alive during the surgery. Doctors remove the diseased heart, and then transplant the donor heart into the patient's body during a procedure that takes from four to six hours. Finally, the patient is removed from the bypass machine. Once the doctors get the new heart beating, the patient is on the road to recovery.

aorta

pulmonay artery

pulmonay valve

mitral valve

superior vena cava

right atrium

tricuspid valve

Each part of the human heart must work perfectly. A donated heart will not be accepted if it is damaged.

right ventrical

cardiac muscle

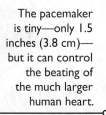

The pacemaker is tiny—only 1.5 inches (3.8 cm)—but it can control the beating of the much larger human heart.

Keeping the Beat

When the heart cannot keep a constant, pulsing rhythm, the problem is called **arrhythmia**. Millions of healthy people experience this every once in a while. But when it happens a lot, it is a serious problem. Then doctors will install a pacemaker near the patient's heart. Electrodes run from the battery-operated device directly into the heart. Whenever the pacemaker doesn't sense a regular heartbeat, it gives the **ventricles** of the heart a very mild electric pulse to keep it pumping in rhythm.

Inside Knowledge

Did you know the heart pumps 2.5 billion times in an average lifetime? Every day, it pumps 6 quarts (5.7 liters) of blood around 12,000 miles (19,312 km).

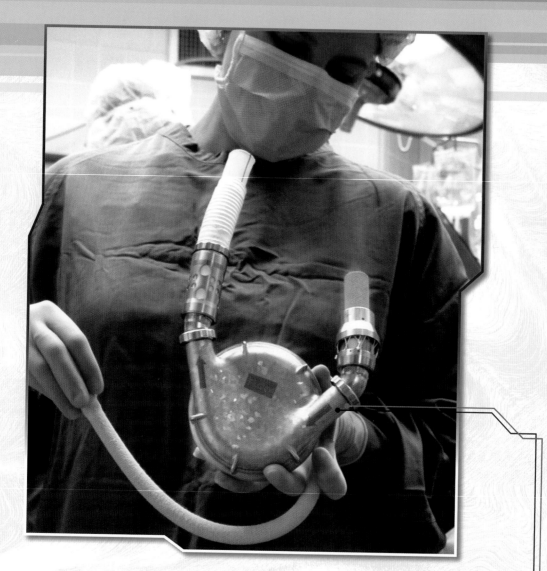

Not Enough Hearts

More than two thousand successful heart transplants are performed every year in the United States. However, thousands more Americans have to wait for donors. Most of those patients stay alive with the help of artificial parts or machines. The Ventricle Assist Device (VAD) helps keep a damaged heart pumping.

The VAD is inserted under the skin and tissue of the upper belly wall. Tubes connect the pump to the heart and the aorta. Another tube passes outside the body and connects to the battery and controller. Tubes are connected to a pump that sits outside the patient's body. The pump makes sure blood gets to the lungs and circulatory system.

This Thoratec HeartMate VE is a pump that is implanted in the patient's chest. It does the work of the left ventricle.

Bionic Hearts

Sometimes even a VAD isn't enough, and a donor heart isn't available. Another solution is needed.

For a long time, there was no other solution. Then, in 1982, Barney Clark became the first person to receive a completely artificial heart. Called the Jarvik-7, the bulky device kept Clark alive for 112 days. The sixth patient to get a Jarvik heart lived nearly two years.

Today, there is a new artificial heart that shows promise. The AbioCor Heart is implanted completely inside the patient's chest. A small battery keeps it pumping. The AbioCor was first tested in 2001, and a later model was introduced in 2009.

The AbioCor implantable is the first totally implantable artificial heart.

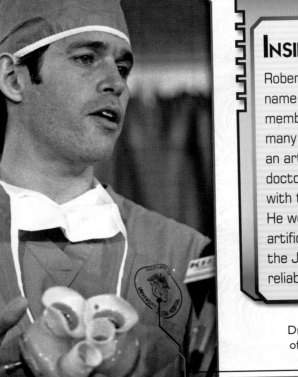

Inside Knowledge

Robert Jarvik's famous heart has his name even though he was just one member of a team. Jarvik was one of many graduate students working on an artificial heart project for another doctor, and Jarvik's team came up with the best idea. The name stuck. He would go on to create other artificial parts for the heart, including the Jarvik 2000, one of the most reliable VADs to date.

Dr. Robert Jarvik holds a model of a heart like the one that was implanted in Barney Clark.

Cows and Pigs to the Rescue

Scientists have also been able to help heart patients with transplants from some unlikely sources: animals. Scientists have discovered that the hearts of pigs and cows are very similar to those of humans. So, when the heart valves that control the flow of blood are damaged in humans, doctors can transplant similar valves from cows and pigs. The valves are treated with chemicals attached to metal and cloth frames and sewn into the heart. Both cow and pig valves usually last ten to fifteen years inside a human body.

Fake Blood and Synthetic Vessels

Human blood is very complex. This is why scientists have not been able to develop true artificial blood. However, there are synthetic, or manufactured, liquids that can help a patient in need of blood. One type makes it seem like there is more blood in a person's body than there actually is. Another type helps to keep the oxygen levels in the blood at a healthy level.

Researchers have had greater success creating artificial blood vessels. Plastic and rubber are the most common type of artificial vessels used in humans. They have been used since the 1950s. Newer developments include a hybrid vessel that is made from a combination of plastic and blood vessel cells taken from humans. There are also experiments underway to grow completely new vessels from human cells alone.

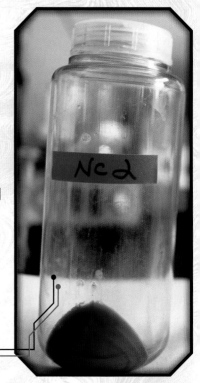

Scientists have discovered a way to use bacterial cells to create hemoglobin, the oxygen-carrying molecule in the blood. The vial on the bottom shows the red color that indicates that the molecules are doing their job.

Baby Fae

Baby Fae is seen at Loma Linda University Medical Center, November 1984.

In 1984, doctors tried an astonishing surgery on a little girl known only as Baby Fae. The baby had been born with a fatal heart defect. She would have died within days.

No human donor hearts were available, and doctors did not yet know that cow and pig hearts were the most compatible organs. So doctors decided to try to give her the heart of a baboon. This exact procedure had never been tried before. After a four-hour surgery, Baby Fae's new heart began to beat on its own.

The whole nation was fascinated by Baby Fae's story. Some thought the little girl's doctor and parents were acting courageously. Others felt it was wrong to experiment on a baby. In any case, Baby Fae's body rejected the baboon heart after twenty-one days, and she died. However, her experience has inspired others to keep looking for unusual answers to difficult problems.

ORGAN REPLACEMENT

Heart transplants are dramatic, but they aren't the most common kind of transplant. Other organs are replaced far more often.

Kidney, liver, and pancreas transplants are common procedures in many hospitals. They are also among the most successful types of transplants.

The Mighty Kidney

Every day, our kidneys sift out waste products from about 50 gallons (189 l) of blood. We get rid of that waste when we urinate. When kidneys are damaged, they may stop filtering the waste. This can make a person very sick. There are two ways doctors treat damaged kidneys.

With **dialysis**, a machine is used in place of the damaged kidneys to keep the blood clean. In the most common type of dialysis, blood is extracted from the person's body, cleaned, and returned. Dialysis must be done at least several times a week.

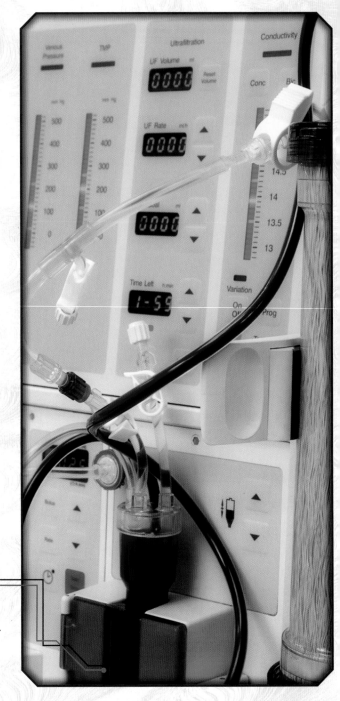

A dialysis machine functions as an artificial kidney, cleaning the blood.

A kidney transplant is another treatment option. People can live full lives with only one healthy kidney. But if both are damaged, then a new organ is needed. Siblings make the best donors, since their bodies contain much of the same DNA.

Once a donor organ is found, the transplant operation takes only a few hours. The biggest challenge in these transplants is keeping the body from rejecting the new kidney. The body's immune system is trained to fight foreign invaders. When a new organ is placed in the body, the immune system kicks into high gear. Patients must take drugs to help treat this reaction.

A kidney is prepared for transplant. It can survive outside the body for forty-eight to sixty-two hours.

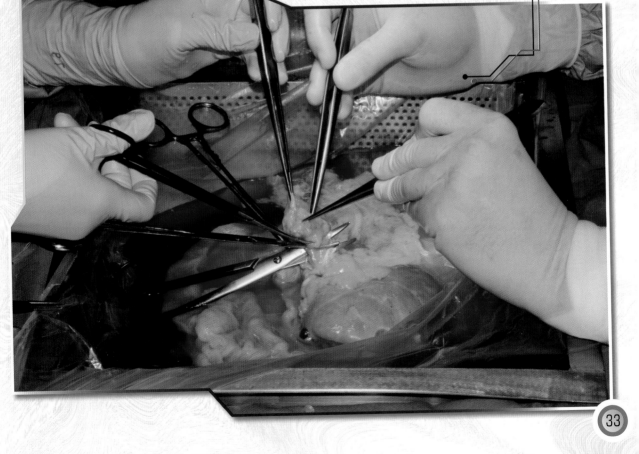

The Liver: Big and Busy

The liver is the biggest organ in the body, other than the skin. It converts food into nutrients, stores fats and sugars for later use, produces **bile**, and cleans out harmful chemicals that get into the body. When a liver is diseased or damaged, doctors will sometimes transplant a complete liver from a donor. They may also perform partial transplants, in which only part of a liver is used. Partial transplants are usually performed on children and are successful because the liver is the only internal organ that can **regenerate**, meaning it can grow back some of what has been lost.

A healthy adult liver is about the size of a small football.

duodenum
(intestine)

pancreas

The pancreas is about
6 inches (15.2 cm)
long. It is positioned
behind the stomach.

The Curious Pancreas

The pancreas may be small, but it plays a key role in digesting food and maintaining **insulin** levels in the blood. Patients with severe diabetes—a disease in which a person's insulin levels are out of whack—can develop problems including blindness and kidney failure. A pancreas transplant can help control insulin levels and prevent problems. But there are other treatments that can help people with less severe cases of diabetes. There's even a nifty monitoring device that acts as an artificial pancreas! It monitors insulin levels and lets users know when they need more insulin.

INSIDE KNOWLEDGE

When an organ is donated, it must be quickly transferred to the waiting patient. That's because organs can only survive outside the body for a certain amount of time:

- Heart and lungs: 4–6 hours
- Kidneys: 48–62 hours
- Liver: 12–24 hours
- Pancreas: 12-24 hours

Limited Organs and Long Lists

The United Network for Organ Sharing (UNOS) is a national organization that acts as the hub for all organ donations. UNOS keeps an amazing database that contains critical details about each waiting patient and about every organ donated.

So how does the process work?
1. Patients approved for a transplant are put on a waiting list.
2. When an organ is donated, all vital information is patched into the database.
3. A patient is chosen to receive the organ, based on these factors:
   - who is closest to where the donated organ is
   - who is the best match for the organ
   - who has been on the list longest for that type of organ
   - who would benefit most from the transplant

Some patients wait years for a donated organ. Others wait only weeks. But the UNOS system is trusted because it is fair. No one is given preference based on wealth or fame.

HUMAN ORGAN

Organs are placed in sterile containers and packaged in wet ice. They are then hand-delivered to the recipient's treatment center.

INSIDE KNOWLEDGE

On an average twenty-four-hour day at the UNOS Organ Center, six organ placement specialists during two twelve-hour shifts will:

- place, or attempt to place, fifteen organs for transplantation
- process and transmit twelve organ donor matches to waiting OPOs (Organ Procurement Organizations)
- receive 350 telephone requests from transplant centers, OPOs, and laboratories
- spend more than twenty-six work-hours placing organs and communicating matching information

Chris Klug

Chris Klug was competing professionally just four months after his liver transplant.

Born in Vail, Colorado, Chris Klug began snowboarding at a very early age. By age sixteen, he was already competing professionally. Then, at twenty-two, he got what seemed to be a flu that would not go away. The "flu" turned out to be cholangitis, a disease that scars the bile ducts. Klug needed a new liver.

Klug was on the transplant waiting list for six years. Finally, he got the call: a new liver was waiting for him.

Just weeks after the transplant, Klug resumed training. He won a World Cup race six months later and then the bronze medal at the 2002 Olympics. Now one of Klug's main goals is to raise awareness about transplants. He does this through the Chris Klug Foundation, and supporters whom he calls the Donor Dudes.

ARTIFICIAL BONES

Human bones are super-tough. Even when they break, they heal to become almost as strong as they were before. One challenge for researchers has been to find a replacement substance that's as good as the original.

Scientists have already developed one solution: an injectable bone that looks like toothpaste. It can be inserted directly into the area of a bone that needs repair. It can't really match the strength of a healthy human bone, but the injectable bone does harden, and it allows the healing bone and tissues to grow normally around it.

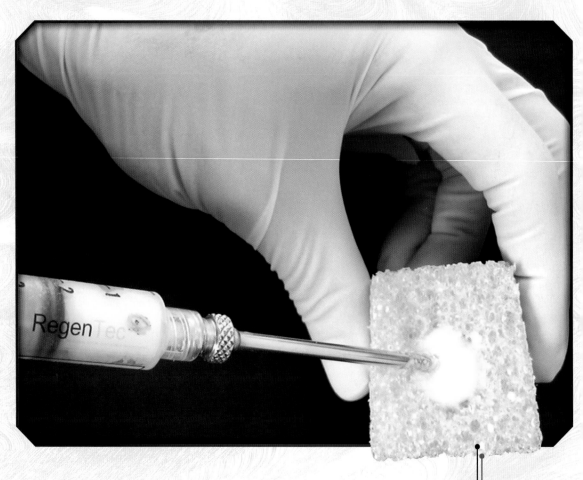

Injectable bone substitute is very effective in healing fractures of the vertebrae—the bones in the spine.

Portions of the jaw or skull are sometimes weakened or destroyed by disease. Polymer substitutes can replace the damaged pieces.

Injections and Inkjet Printers

Researchers have been using polymers, or plastics, to create artificial bones for many years. But recent developments may soon revolutionize the way polymer bones are made. Here's how the new process would work:

- a patient's X ray, or **CT scan**, is fed into a computer to make a three-dimensional (3-D) model of the bone that needs to be replaced
- the 3-D model is sliced into thin layers, and the data is sent to a 3-D inkjet printer
- the printer then "prints out" layers of polymer, one on top of the other. When the layers are combined, the result is a complete plastic version of the bone.

These types of bones can't hold a lot of weight, so they aren't being used yet for leg bones. But because they can be made to order for patients, they are extremely valuable in facial reconstruction. Cheekbones, jawbones, and even the larger sections of the skull can be made this way.

Skeletons on the Outside

Marvel Comics superhero Iron Man has one. So do scorpions, turtles, and lobsters. Soon, modern military personnel will have them, too. What are we talking about? Exoskeletons. Exoskeletons are hard coverings worn outside the body as a means of protection. The idea is to protect softer tissues and bones from damage with a hard, resistant covering.

The *Star Wars* soldiers created by director George Lucas wear complete exoskeletons. The idea was not lost on military developers looking to create protective gear for soldiers of the future.

Then and Now

Medieval Knights and Darth Vader

Exoskeletons are a pretty old idea. Ancient warriors wore thick leather coverings over their bodies to protect themselves. Medieval knights dressed in heavy iron armor to shield themselves in battle. In the futuristic space world George Lucas created for *Star Wars*, the Evil Empire's soldiers are completely covered in exoskeletons.

Military designers are the ones creating these exoskeletons. The equipment is relatively lightweight and very robotic-looking. It is usually attached to the arms and legs. The exoskeletons will assist the soldiers in their movements, making them stronger and faster. In battle, being able to carry heavier backpacks, lift heavy weapons, run fast for long distances, and jump over large obstacles would make a nearly superhuman soldier.

Exoskeletons also have non-military uses. They can help patients who have to learn to walk again or move their arms after an accident or a stroke. They can also help nurses and doctors more easily lift and move large patients or patients who are **paralyzed**.

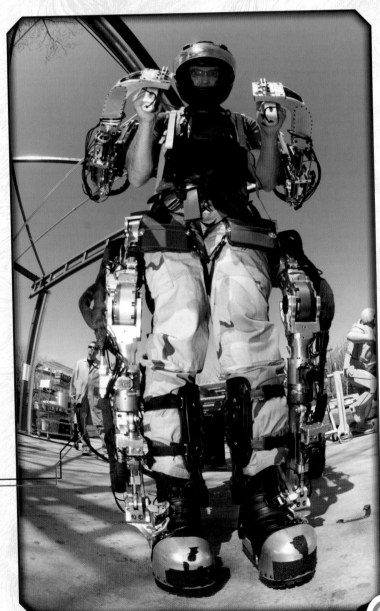

This kind of exoskeleton helps soldiers carry heavy equipment. Think of it as a robotic covering that makes a person stronger and faster.

FRONTIERS OF SCIENCE

Improvements in organ transplants, prosthetic limbs, and artificial body parts are helping people live longer and fuller lives. So, what does the future hold?

Brain Implants Are Here

It sounds like science fiction, but it's true: we can now computerize the human brain. BrainGate is a tiny brain-computer interface that is implanted in a patient's brain and connected to a computer. Simply by thinking, the patient can make his or her brain "talk" with the computer. The computer then does what it is asked. BrainGate is especially valuable to patients who are partially or completely paralyzed.

A patient with a Braingate implant simply thinks about the image on a computer screen that he or she wants the computer's cursor to point to. Braingate's sensors pick up those electrical signals and send them to the computer. The cursor moves to the chosen application and turns it on.

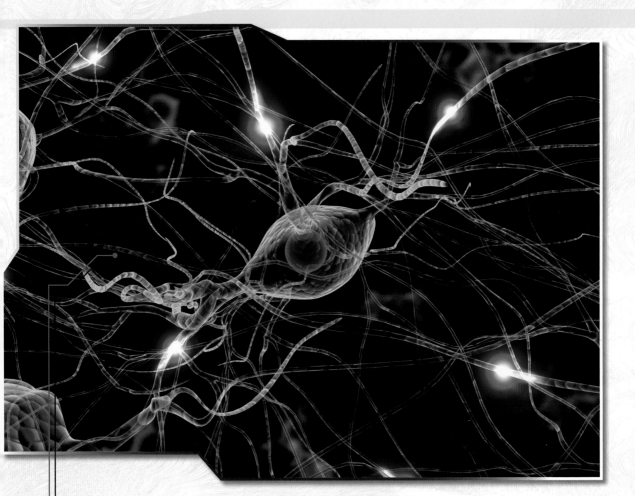

Electrodes can be used to track nerve impulses in the brain so that faulty connections can be addressed.

Using BrainGate, paralyzed patients are able to turn on lights, read e-mails, and move their motorized wheelchairs—just by thinking! If combined with some of the technology that is already available for bionic limbs, BrainGate could make it possible for paralyzed patients to actually move their limbs once again.

INSIDE KNOWLEDGE

Nanobots are minuscule robots that are programmed to perform specific functions. Scientists are experimenting with making nanobots from human DNA and programming them to do things like fight infectious diseases or clean out clogged arteries. They would be injected directly into the bloodstream. Nanobots are still in the early stages of development, but they may change the way patients are treated in the future.

Worms Can—Why Not Humans?

If you cut a worm in half, the missing piece will grow back. What if humans could regenerate? At Wake Forest University in North Carolina, Dr. Anthony Atala has been able to use human cells to create functioning human body parts. Dr. Atala and his team grow the cells in a petri dish. When there are enough cells, they are placed on a three-dimensional scaffold shaped like the organ being engineered. Once it is inside the body, the scaffold slowly dissolves as the cells form tissue and integrate with the body. The first patients to use these organs were seven young children who received bladder implants from Dr. Atala. After an average of five years of follow-up, all the kids were healthy and doing fine.

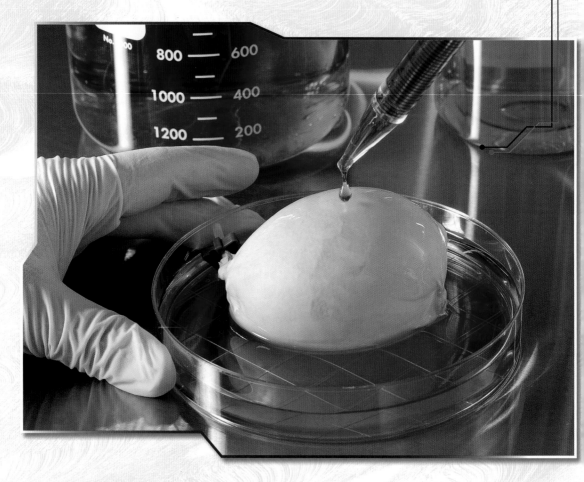

This bladder was grown in a laboratory from the patient's own cells.

Stem cells can make any one of the 220 different types of cells in the human body. They also have the ability to reproduce themselves many times over.

Customized Cells

Stem cells are cells that have the amazing ability to divide and become any other kind of cell in the human body, like blood or heart or muscle cells. This makes them very valuable to scientists looking for cures for a variety of damaging diseases. For example, scientists are having great success using stem cells to repair nerve damage in rats. If this technique works on humans, it could offer amazing possibilities for people who are paralyzed as a result of accidents or strokes.

INSIDE KNOWLEDGE

Swedish scientists have begun creating robotic nerves that respond to the same chemical impulses that real nerves use. These artificial nerves could one day be part of a bionic brain prosthesis. These devices could help victims of stroke or mental illness. They could even create a pathway between our biological brains and our computers!

GLOSSARY

abrasion A scraped or worn area of skin.

arrhythmia A change or skip in the heart's regular rhythm.

bile A fluid produced by the liver that helps in breaking down fats.

bionic Artificial electronic replacement body parts.

collagen A human protein found in skin, bone, and muscles.

CT scan A computerized digital picture that can show sections or slices of the body.

dialysis A system for removing waste or toxins from blood when the kidneys can no longer do it themselves.

impulse A chemical change in a nerve.

insulin A protein created in the pancreas that regulates blood sugar.

myoelectricity The electrical impulses created by human muscles.

nanotechnology The science of creating molecule and atom-sized computer devices.

organic Relating to bodily organs or natural systems.

paralyzed Unable to move one's body parts.

prostheses Artificial devices used to replace human body parts.

regenerate To grow new tissue or body parts.

ventricle A chamber in the heart that receives blood and pushes it into the arteries of the body.

Find Out More

Books

Braga, Newton. *Bionics for the Evil Genius: 25 Build-It-Yourself Projects*. New York: McGraw Hill/TAB Electronics, 2005. A colorful guide to doing simple experiments based on bionic science. This book explains the complex science with clear text and illustrations.

Schwartz, Tina P. *Organ Transplants: A Survival Guide for the Entire Family*. New York: The Scarecrow Press, Inc., 2005. A wide-ranging look at the entire process of organ donation for families of donors and recipients presented in question and answer form.

Walker, Richard. *Dr. Frankenstein's Human Body Book*. New York: DK Publishing, 2008. Join Dr. Frankenstein as he puts together a human body part by part with the help of colorful pages and a fun presentation of the science involved.

Websites

http://discovermagazine.com/
Discover is often the first consumer magazine to report on the latest cutting-edge technologies in medicine and science. The magazine's vast archives are great for research.

www.pbs.org/saf/1107/index.html
"The Bionic Body" is an episode from the Public Broadcasting System's *Scientific American Frontiers* series. The site covers custom-made body parts, electronic eyes, stem cell research, and brain technologies.

www.unos.org/
The United Network for Organ Sharing is a rich resource with information about how organ transplants are done, how the UNOS list works, lifestyle issue for organ recipients, and lots more.

INDEX